Be a SPACE DETECTIVE

Written by

Anita Ganeri

Illustrated by

Paul Doherty

CONTENTS

Derrydale Books

New York

How did it all begin?

The stars, planets, galaxies, and the space around them form the **Universe**. No one knows how big the Universe is. The furthest astronomers can see is about 15,000 million light years, or 885,000 million million million miles! But the Universe probably stretches much, much farther than that!

Most astronomers believe that the Universe began about 15,000 million years ago in a gigantic explosion, called the **"Big Bang."** A tiny cluster of energy blew apart, scattering hot gases out into space. The galaxies formed from this material. No one knows what happened before the Big Bang.

EXPANDING AND SHRINKING

The Universe is still growing with the force of the Big Bang. Some astronomers think it will shrink again, then explode in another Big Bang in about 65,000 million years time. They think that this cycle of expanding then shrinking will be repeated every 80,000 million years. This is just one theory about the state of the Universe. It is called the **Oscillating Universe theory**.

STEADY STATE

Other scientists believe that, although the Universe is still growing, its appearance will never change. They think that new parts of the Universe are still being created from material in space. These parts form at the center of the Universe and replace the parts that are moving outward at the edges of the Universe. This is called the **Steady State theory**.

GALAXIES

Galaxies are giant clouds of stars, which probably formed about 1,000 million years after the Big Bang. Our solar system lies in a galaxy called the **Milky Way**. The Milky Way contains at least 100,000 million stars and measures about 590,000 million million miles across. **Do you know what type of galaxy the Milky Way is?** The nearest galaxy to ours is the **Andromeda Spiral**, about 2.2 light years, or 13 million million miles away.

An elliptical galaxy

A spiral galaxy

A barred spiral galaxy

Light years away

The Universe is so huge that astronomers have to use a special unit, called a light year, to measure it. Light travels at the fastest known speed in the Universe – 186, 171 miles per second. A light year is the distance light travels in one year, that is 5.9 million million miles. **Here are some light year problems for you to solve**:

1. The **Milky Way** is 590,000 million million miles wide. **How many light years is this?**
2. Our next nearest star after the Sun is called **Proxima Centauri**. It is 4.25 light years away. **Can you calculate how many miles this is?**
3. The **Sun** is just over 8 light *minutes* away from Earth. **How many miles is this?**
4. **Pluto** is 5.5 light *hours* away from Earth. **How many miles is this?**

Our Solar System

Our Solar System is made up of the Sun and the nine planets that circle it. In order of their closeness to the Sun, the planets are Mercury, Venus, Earth, Mars, Jupiter, Saturn, Uranus, Neptune, and Pluto. The Sun's light takes over 8 minutes to reach the Earth. It takes 11 hours to reach Pluto. Scientists think that the planets formed about 4,600 million years ago from balls of hot gas.

Everything in the Solar System is moving. The planets spin on their **axes** and circle the Sun. In turn, the planets have moons that circle around them.

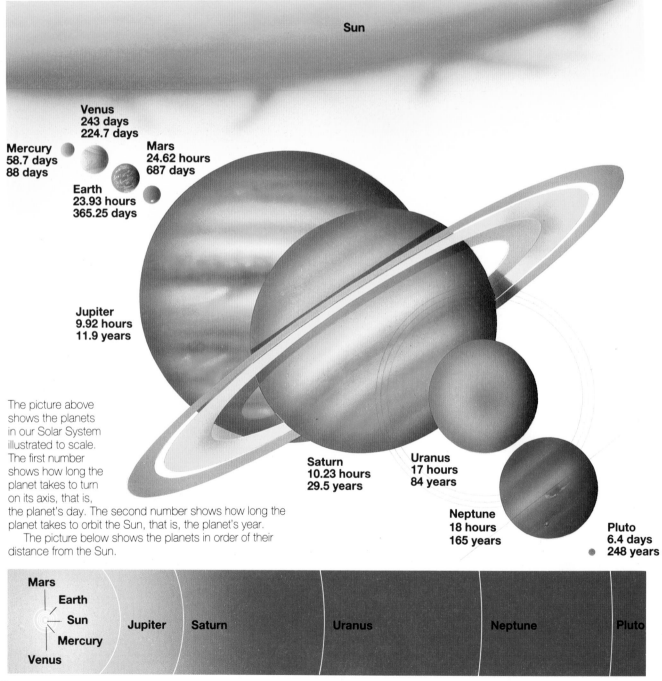

Sun

Venus
243 days
224.7 days

Mercury
58.7 days
88 days

Mars
24.62 hours
687 days

Earth
23.93 hours
365.25 days

Jupiter
9.92 hours
11.9 years

Saturn
10.23 hours
29.5 years

Uranus
17 hours
84 years

Neptune
18 hours
165 years

Pluto
6.4 days
248 years

The picture above shows the planets in our Solar System illustrated to scale. The first number shows how long the planet takes to turn on its axis, that is, the planet's day. The second number shows how long the planet takes to orbit the Sun, that is, the planet's year.

The picture below shows the planets in order of their distance from the Sun.

Mars
Earth
Sun
Mercury
Venus
Jupiter
Saturn
Uranus
Neptune
Pluto

THE SUN

Without the **Sun**, there would be no life on Earth. But the Sun is just one of many millions of stars in our galaxy. It is not la very big star even though it measures almost 900,000 miles across. The Sun is mainly made up of hydrogen gas. It burns up about 700 tons of hydrogen a second in the *nuclear reactions* which create its heat and light. The temperature of the Sun's surface is about 15,000°F. At the center it rises to an amazing 59 million°F!

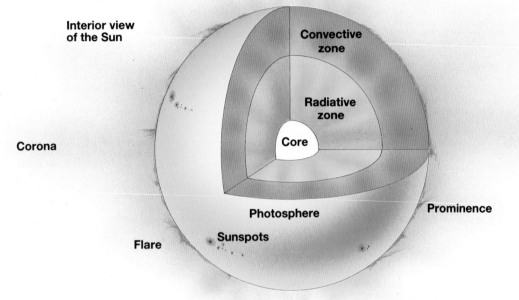

Interior view of the Sun

Convective zone

Radiative zone

Core

Corona

Photosphere

Sunspots

Flare

Prominence

Looking for sunspots

Dark patches, called **sunspots**, sometimes appear on the Sun. They are patches of gas which are cooler than the rest of the surface. As a Space Detective you can see the sunspots for yourself. You will need a pair of binoculars (with a magnification of 12 or less) and two large pieces of white cardboard.

1. Cut a hole out of one of the pieces of cardboard, as shown. The rest of the cardboard must cover the other half of the binoculars. This is your shield.

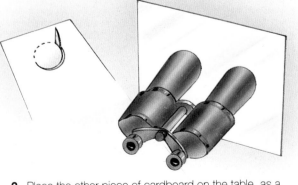

2. Place the other piece of cardboard on the table, as a screen. Point the binoculars toward the Sun and focus them so that the Sun's image appears on your screen.

3. You can alter the size of the image by moving your binoculars closer to or farther away from the screen.

4. Draw the pattern of spots you see each day, and watch out for new ones appearing. Keep a record of how they change over several months. Your drawings may look like those below.

NEVER LOOK DIRECTLY AT THE SUN!

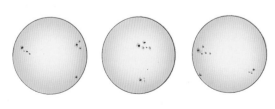

The planets

The four planets closest to the Sun are called the inner planets. They are Mercury, Venus, Earth, and Mars. These planets are rocky, with mainly dry surfaces. Four of the outer planets, Jupiter, Saturn, Uranus, and Neptune, are very different. They have small rocky centers, surrounded by layers of gas. The farthest planet from the Sun, Pluto, is a small, solid planet.

So far, life has only been discovered on one planet, the Earth.

THE INNER PLANETS

Mercury Because it is so close to the Sun, Mercury is scorching hot during the day. Temperatures reach 950°F. Mercury has no atmosphere to trap heat. Therefore, at night, temperatures plummet to -626°F.

Earth The Earth receives just enough heat and light from the Sun to support life. Nearly three-quarters of planet Earth is covered in water.

Venus Venus is so bright that you can see it without a telescope. Look out for it in the evening. Venus is surrounded by poisonous carbon dioxide gas and swirling clouds of sulfuric acid. At 1184°F, it is even hotter than Mercury.

Mars Mars is called the red planet because of the color of its rocky surface. The sky is also colored pink by red dust blown into the atmosphere.

★ **ANSWERS** ★

SPOT THE PLANETS

1. Mars	4. Earth	7. Mercury
2. Uranus	5. Pluto	8. Venus
3. Jupiter	6. Saturn	9. Neptune

These planets are not drawn to scale

THE OUTER PLANETS

Jupiter Jupiter is the biggest planet. It is about 11 times wider than the Earth. The huge red patch on Jupiter's side is called its **Great Red Spot**. This is a vast cloud of wind and whirling gas.

Saturn Saturn is surrounded by beautiful rings, made up of millions of rock and ice fragments. They form a series of thin bands, each only a few miles wide.

Neptune Neptune is very similar to Uranus, although it is slightly smaller. Like Uranus, Neptune looks green because of the methane in its atmosphere.

Uranus Uranus looks green from Earth because of methane gas in its atmosphere. The narrow rings surrounding Uranus were only discovered in 1977.

These planets are not drawn to scale

Pluto Pluto is the smallest planet in our Solar System and the furthest away from the Sun. It is far too cold to support any life. Pluto was the last planet to be discovered, in 1930.

Spot the planets

Imagine that you are traveling through the Solar System. Would you recognize the different planets? Here are some clues to help you identify them. **To which planet does each refer?**

1. Planet of pink skies?
2. Ringed in green?
3. A windy spot!
4. The water planet?
5. Last but not least?
6. Ice rings?
7. Scorching hot?
8. Cloudy skies?
9. Green again?

Space wanderers

The planets and their moons are not the only objects that circle around the Sun. Other space wanderers in our Solar System include asteroids, comets, meteors, and meteorites.

Asteroids are small, irregular planets of rock and metal. They are leftovers from the formation of the planets, and they lie in the asteroid belt between Mars and Jupiter. Comets are balls of ice and dust that travel around the Sun, glowing with the Sun's light. Meteors are small lumps of space rock that may come from a comet's tail. Meteorites are larger chunks of rock, which may come from comets or asteroids.

1. Sun
2. Mars
3. Comet
4. Halley's comet
5. Asteroid belt
6. Jupiter

ASTEROIDS

There are about 40,000 asteroids in orbit in the asteroid belt. Many are only the size of soccer balls. They were unknown until 1801, when the biggest, called Ceres, was discovered. Ceres is 621 miles wide and moves around the Sun every 4.6 years. Scientists think that asteroids may be pieces of material left over from the time when the Solar System was formed.

COMETS

There may be as many as 100,000 million comets circling the Sun. When a comet gets close to the Sun, a long tail streams behind it. The tail is made of dust and gases released from the comet by the Sun's heat. The tail is blown away from the Sun by solar winds. The Great Comet of 1843 had a tail about 205 million miles long!

SHOOTING STARS

When **meteors** enter the Earth's atmosphere, they burn up in the sky. This produces a streak of light, called a "shooting star." Meteors can appear at any time and from any direction. At certain times of the year, though, they appear in groups, called *showers*. The part of the sky from which they come is called the *radiant*.

METEORITES

Meteorites fall to Earth without burning up. They sometimes leave huge craters, such as the Arizona Crater, shown below. It was formed some 22,000 years ago by a meteorite hitting the Earth with a force equal to a thousand atomic bombs. The largest known meteorite is made of iron and weighs about 60 tons.

Meteor watching

The best time to watch for meteors is on a clear, moonless night. You don't need any special equipment – just a reclining sun chair, a sleeping bag or blanket, a notepad and pen, and a watch. Choose a time when a meteor shower is expected (see the list on the right). Then lie back, wait, and watch. You need to watch for at least an hour. If you are with a group of friends, each of you should watch a different part of the sky. Don't forget to make a note of how many meteors you see, and when they appear.

MAJOR METEOR SHOWERS

Quadrantids January 1-6
April Lyrids April 19-24
Perseids July 25-Aug 18

Orionids October 16-26
Geminids December 7-15

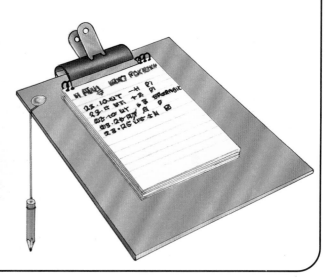

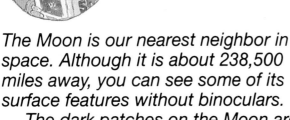

The face of the moon

The Moon is our nearest neighbor in space. Although it is about 238,500 miles away, you can see some of its surface features without binoculars.

The dark patches on the Moon are called seas. They do not contain water but were covered in volcanic lava millions of years ago. The brighter patches are the highlands, which cover three-quarters of the Moon. The surface is also pitted with craters, formed by meteorites.

The Moon is a completely silent place because there is no air to carry sounds. There is no wind to blow dust over the footprints left by the Apollo astronauts. They will probably not disappear for another ten million years.

* * ANSWERS * *

BE A MOON SLEUTH

1. There is no air on the Moon. So there is no wind to wear things away or cover them with dust or soil.
2. The craters were formed by meteorites crashing into the Moon's surface. The Arizona crater in the United States was made by a meteorite.
3. We can only see the Moon because the Sun shines on it, and the sunlight is then reflected down to Earth.
4. It takes the Moon 29.5 days to pass through all its phases.
5. The seas do not contain water. They are covered in ancient volcanic lava. In contrast to the Moon, nearly three-quarters of the Earth is covered with water.

CHANGING SHAPE

The **Moon** takes 27.3 days to orbit the Earth. During this time, it seems to change shape from a sliver to a full circle. This is because we can see different amounts of the sunlit side of the Moon as it travels around us. The changing shapes are called the phases of the Moon. The Moon takes 29.5 days to pass through its phases.

From Earth, we always see the same side of the Moon. No one had ever seen the "dark side" of the Moon until 1959. Then the Soviet **Luna 3** spacecraft flew behind the Moon and took photographs of the other side.

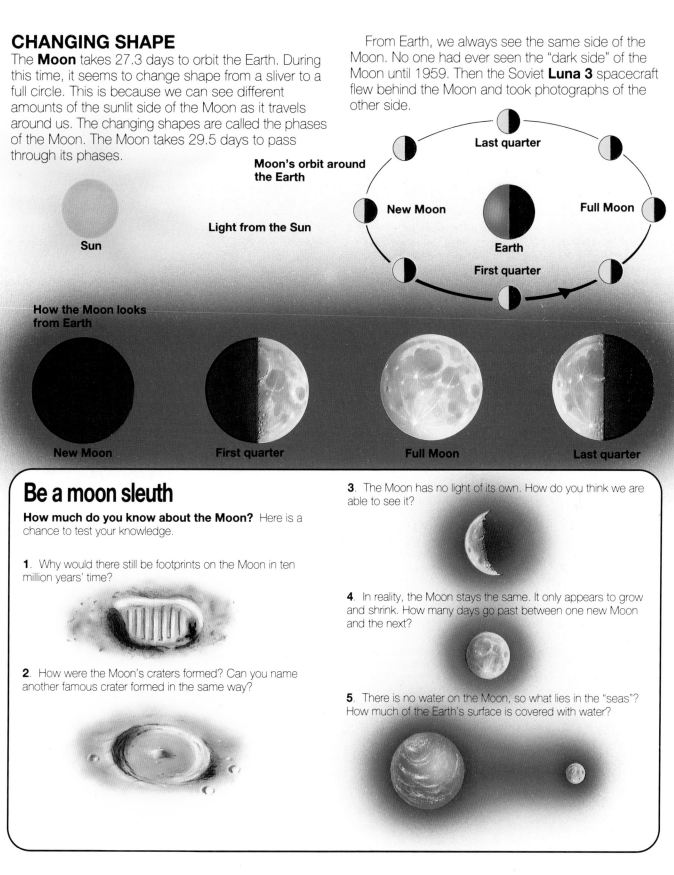

Moon's orbit around the Earth

Sun

Light from the Sun

Last quarter

New Moon

Full Moon

Earth

First quarter

How the Moon looks from Earth

New Moon   **First quarter**   **Full Moon**   **Last quarter**

Be a moon sleuth

How much do you know about the Moon? Here is a chance to test your knowledge.

1. Why would there still be footprints on the Moon in ten million years' time?

2. How were the Moon's craters formed? Can you name another famous crater formed in the same way?

3. The Moon has no light of its own. How do you think we are able to see it?

4. In reality, the Moon stays the same. It only appears to grow and shrink. How many days go past between one new Moon and the next?

5. There is no water on the Moon, so what lies in the "seas"? How much of the Earth's surface is covered with water?

The life of a star

A star is a huge, glowing ball of mainly hydrogen gas. This is held together by the star's own gravity. In the center of the star, **nuclear reactions** convert the gas into heat and light energy. Stars make their own light, unlike planets, which only reflect light from stars.

Stars come in a range of sizes. At one end of the scale are giants such as Betelgeuse, which is 621 million miles across. At the other are stars, such as Sirius, which is only a few thousand miles wide.

STAR BIRTH AND DEATH

Stars are born in huge clouds of dust and gas, called *nebulae*. A small lump of the cloud breaks off. It gets smaller and hotter, until nuclear reactions start in the center and a star is born. In a star's center the temperature may reach 61 million°F.

When a star has used up all its fuel, it starts to die. It swells up into a huge **red giant** star. The next stage in some larger stars is a giant explosion, a **supernova**, which blasts most of the star's material out into space. The outcome of a supernova is either a **neutron star**, which is very small and heavy, or a **black hole** (see page 15).

Find the Galaxy

Below you can see pictures of the **North American Nebula**, the **Andromeda Galaxy** and a group of stars, called the **Pleiades**. **Can you determine which is which? Can you remember what the difference between a nebula and a galaxy is?**

3.

2.

1.

1. Nebula
2. Red giant
3. Supernova
4. Neutron star
5. Black hole

WHITE DWARF

When smaller stars cool down, they too expand to become red giants. The cool outer layers are lost and the center collapses into a small, heavy **white dwarf**, about the size of our Earth. A white dwarf is made of nuclear ash, which weighs one ton a teaspoonful.

BLACK HOLES

Some of the more massive stars end in a different way. They first become a neutron star. Their *gravity* is then so strong that they are sucked back into a **black hole**. Here the pull of gravity is so strong that not even light can escape from the hole.

The Orion Nebula

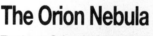

The huge **Orion Nebula** glows so brightly you can see it without the help of a telescope, although it is about 1,600 light years away. It looks like a misty patch in the sky. You can find it by first locating the stars which make up the belt of the Orion constellation (see pages 16 and 17).

dust and gas, from which stars are born.
3. **North American Nebula.** A nebula is a huge cloud of
2. **Andromeda Galaxy.** A galaxy is a giant cloud of stars.
seven of the brightest stars with the naked eye.
also called the Seven Sisters because you can often see
1. The **Pleiades** are a cluster of over 200 stars. They are
FIND THE GALAXY

★ ANSWERS ★

Mapping the heavens

Watching the stars is a must for all Space Detectives. Many stars form patterns which make them easy to recognize. These are called **constellations**. They often have Latin or Greek names. Look at the same part of the sky at the same time each evening. You will see different stars throughout the year, as the Earth moves in its orbit around the Sun.

The stars on these two pages are visible in the **Northern Hemisphere**.

ORION

In Greek mythology, **Orion** was a giant and a hunter. Look out for the three stars that make up his belt, then you will be able to find the rest of him.

PEGASUS

In Greek mythology, **Pegasus** was a winged horse that flew through the sky, carrying thunderbolts from the god, Zeus. First look for the square of stars which make up Pegasus's body.

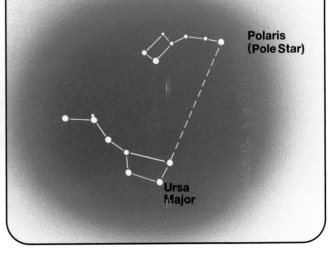

URSA MAJOR

Ursa Major means "great bear" in Latin. The seven brightest stars in this constellation are also known as the **Plow**, because they make a plow shape.

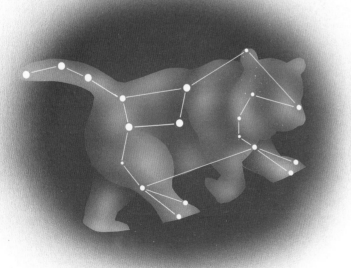

Finding the pole star

The Pole Star, **Polaris**, is one of the brightest stars in the Northern Hemisphere. It is a useful landmark for finding other constellations. Below you can see how to locate the Pole Star. First, you have to find **Ursa Major**.

Polaris
(Pole Star)

Ursa Major

SEEING STARS

Now you can try to find some constellations in the night sky, with the help of the star map below. Start by learning the positions of the brightest stars and main constellations, and use them to help you find the smaller, fainter ones. It is much better to watch stars in the countryside than in the town. A countryside sky is often much darker. In a town, the streetlights make the fainter stars very difficult to see.

You will be able to see many of the stars without using binoculars or a telescope. If you do want to use binoculars, buy a small pair so your arms don't ache while you are holding them up to the sky. Binoculars of size 7x50 are best to start with. They will give you good magnification and will have lots of light-gathering power. Keep a star diary, noting down which stars you have seen and where they appear in the sky from night to night.

The Northern sky

Aries (ram)   Pisces (fish)   Aquarius (water carrier)

Taurus (bull)   Capricornus (horned goat)

Gemini (twins)   Sagittarius (archer)

Cancer (crab)   Scorpius (scorpion)

Leo (lion)   Libra (scales)

Virgo (virgin)

Virgo
Leo
Boötes
Cancer
Ursa Major
(The Plow)
Gemini
Hercules
Orion
Ursa Minor
Draco
Lyra
Polaris (Pole Star)
Milky Way
Taurus
Cassiopeia
Cygnus
Perseus
Andromeda
Aries
Pegasus
Pisces

17

Another sky

People living in the **Southern Hemisphere** see the sky the other way up. In the southern sky there are also plenty of constellations to discover.

There are some very bright stars in the southern half of the sky. A star's brightness is measured in units of magnitude. A bright star is magnitude 1, and the faintest stars are magnitude 6. Each unit of magnitude shows a difference of 2.512 in brightness. Some stars are even brighter than magnitude 1. The brightest star in the sky is Sirius. Its magnitude is –1.43.

CENTAURUS
The constellation of **Centaurus** includes the stars **Alpha Centauri** and **Proxima Centauri**. Proxima Centauri is thought to be the closest star to Earth, after the Sun.

SCORPIUS
Scorpius means "scorpion" in Latin. Can you make out the scorpion's body and tail? One of the stars in Scorpius is called **Antares**. It is a giant star, some 279,450,000 miles wide.

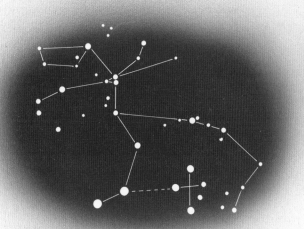

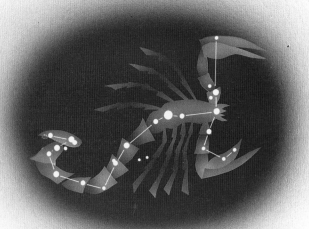

CANIS MAJOR
In Latin, **Canis Major** means "big dog." One of the stars, **Sirius**, is named after Orion's hunting dog and the constellation appears to follow Orion in the sky.

THE SOUTHERN CROSS
Like the Pole Star, the **Southern Cross**, or **Crux**, is a good landmark for spotting other constellations. One of the stars in the Cross, called **Gamma**, has a slight orange-red tint.

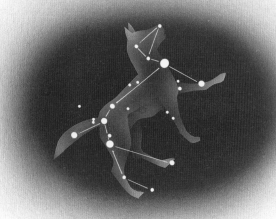

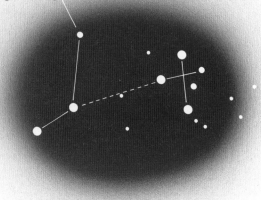

STAR SPOTTING

The star map below will help you to locate and recognize the constellations in the southern sky.

If you decide to buy a telescope to help you spot the stars, a *refracting* telescope is best for beginners. This is a telescope which collects light from the stars using a lens. (A *reflecting* telescope uses a mirror to collect light.) Make sure that the telescope has an *achromatic* lens, which will give you a truer quality of color. Also make sure that the telescope is mounted on a steady *tripod*. Without one, the image will blur every time you move the telescope from one constellation to another. Visiting a planetarium is another good way of learning about the stars.

The Southern sky

The study of space

People have been fascinated by space for thousands of years. In ancient times, people studied the positions of the Moon and Sun to find out the best times to sow or harvest their crops. Early sailors navigated by using the Sun and the stars.

The study of space is called **astronomy**, which means "star naming." The world's first astronomical observatory was probably the Great Pyramid of Cheops, built by the Ancient Egyptians over 4,500 years ago. It doubled as a tomb and a calendar.

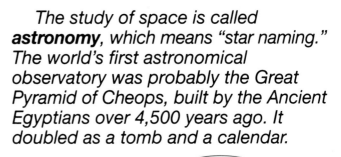

Ptolemy's theory

Copernicus's theory

THE EARLY THEORIES

In about 150 AD, **Ptolemy**, a Greek astronomer, stated that the Earth stood at the center of the Universe. It stayed still, while the Sun, Moon, and the five planets then known (Mercury, Venus, Mars, Jupiter, and Saturn) moved around it.

In 1543, **Nicholas Copernicus**, a Polish clergyman, said that the Sun was at the center of the Solar System, not the Earth. He discovered that all the planets turned on their axes and orbited the Sun.

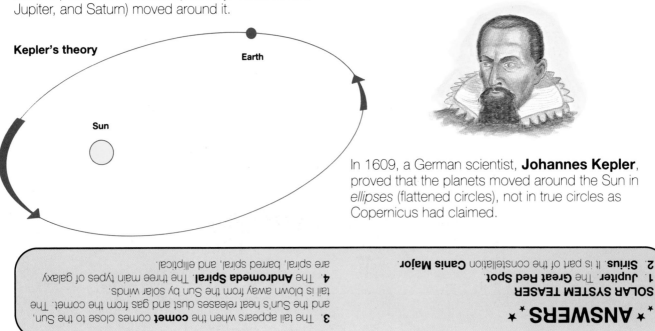

Kepler's theory

Earth

Sun

In 1609, a German scientist, **Johannes Kepler**, proved that the planets moved around the Sun in *ellipses* (flattened circles), not in true circles as Copernicus had claimed.

SKY WATCH

The first person to use a telescope in astronomy was **Galileo Galilei** in the early 17th century. The most powerful telescope today is the **Hubble Space Telescope**. Launched into space from the U.S. **Space Shuttle** in April 1990, it can see seven times further into space than any telescope before it.

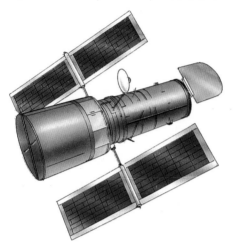

Many modern astronomer's work in special observatories. These are often built high up on mountainsides, above the clouds and away from the glare of streetlights in towns.

Anybody out there?

No one knows if there is life anywhere else in the Universe. But two planetary *probes*, **Pioneer 10** and **Pioneer 11**, carry messages for any aliens they might meet. They have metal plaques, showing sketches of our Solar System and of a man and a woman.

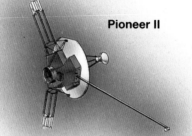

Pioneer II

There have been many reports of people seeing flashing lights, and even flying saucers in the sky. These are known as UFOs, or Unidentified Flying Objects. Some cannot be explained and could be from another planet. Have you seen one yet?

UFO

Solar System teaser

It took early astronomers a long time to figure out a correct picture of our Solar System. **How good is your knowledge about our place in space?**

1. Which is the biggest planet? What is its most famous landmark?
2. Which is the brightest star in the night sky, and which constellation is it part of?

3. When does a comet's tail appear? Why does it always point away from the Sun?
4. Which is the nearest galaxy to ours? Can you name the three main types of galaxy?

Quiz time

Here are some more space puzzles that you can solve by looking back through the book. If you figure out the answers to these, you are well on your way to becoming a great Space Detective.

There are lots of books, television programs, and magazines to help you. You can also visit museums and planetariums. But the simplest way of all is to stand outside and look up!

IDENTITY PARADE
A very important part of being a Space Detective is to be able to tell the difference between one heavenly body and another. Look at the two objects below. **Can you name them?**

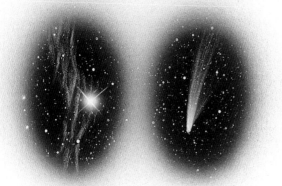

PLANET BIRTHDAYS
Can you recognize the four planets below? How long, in Earth years, would you have to wait between birthdays on each of these planets? Don't forget that a planet's year is the time it takes to travel once around the Sun.

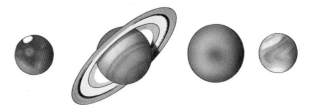

STAR GAZERS
Here are some more constellations to identify. Use the maps on pages 17 and 19 to help you.

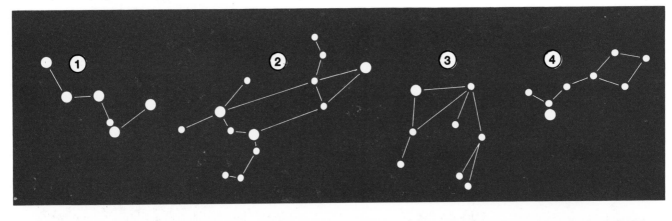

✦ ANSWERS ✦

PLANET BIRTHDAYS
1. On **Mars** you'd have to wait 687 Earth days.
2. On **Saturn** you'd have to wait 29.5 Earth years.
3. On **Uranus** you'd have to wait 85 Earth years.
4. On **Venus** you'd have to wait 224.7 Earth days.

IDENTITY PARADE
1. This is the nebula called the Veil Nebula.
2. This is a comet.

STAR GAZERS
1. Cassiopeia.
2. Leo.
3. Libra.
4. Phoenix.